Usborne
Little Coloring Farm

Illustrated by Jenny Brown

Words by Kate Nolan

Welcome to the farmhouse.

How are you
today, cow?

"Brrm brrrrm!"
goes the tractor.

Cheep, cheep,
little chicks!

Oink!
Muddy puddles are fun.

Isn't the water
nice today?

A friendly
scarecrow

A leaping lamb

All kinds of
vegetables

It's springtime!

Hay for
breakfast...
yum!

Windmills turn on breezy days.

Moving to a new field

This is the
sheepdog.

Where are you going, goose?

A house for the
hens to live in

Good morning,
goat.

Shhh... it's
nap time!

A barn full of hay

Let's go!

Buzz, buzz, buzzzzzzzz

I'm a dragonfly and I love flying!

What a perfect
pumpkin.

Alpacas are
SO fluffy.

Lots of juicy
berries...

...and a carrot
for a bunny

Come for a swim with us, frog!

The apples are
ready to pick.

Cluck! Soon my chicks will hatch.

It's fun to run
among the flowers.

Tu-whit
tu-whooo!